Early China

CONTENTS

Cradle of civilization	4
The origins of China	6
A history of turbulence	8
Imperial life	10
Chang'an	12
City life	14
The peasantry	16
Science and industry	18
Art	20
Belief	22
Family life	24
Preparations for eternity	26
The terracotta army	28
Past and present	30
Glossary	32
Index	32

© Aladdin Books Ltd

Designed and produced by
Aladdin Books Ltd
70 Old Compton Street
London W1

First published in the
United States in 1986 by
Gloucester Press
387 Park Avenue South
New York NY 10016

Printed in Belgium

ISBN 0-531-17025-X

Library of Congress
Catalog Card No. 86-80624

Certain illustrations have previously appeared in the "Civilization Library" series published by Gloucester Press.

The consultant on this book, Frances Wood, is Head of the Chinese Department, British Library, London, England.

THE CIVILIZATION LIBRARY

Early China

DENISE GOFF

Illustrated by
ANGUS McBRIDE, KAREN JOHNSON
AND TERRY DALLEY

Consultant
FRANCES WOOD

Gloucester Press
New York · Toronto · 1986

Cradle of civilization

Chinese civilization first began to emerge in 1600BC, in the valley of the turbulent Yellow River. From this center, despite power battles and invasions by barbarians, the Chinese developed a self-contained culture that has flourished for over 3,500 years.

Geographical setting

The physical environment played a vital role in shaping this culture and in its success. The land of the Yellow River, with its rich earth, droughts and floods, and the Yangtze plain in the south, were bound by formidable natural barriers – mountains, jungle and sea. The Great Wall protected the northern frontier.

These barriers preserved the uniqueness of the Yellow River culture, and the demanding environment they contained influenced the whole Chinese way of life.

Along with the building of the Great Wall, flood control was a major task of the early Chinese. Peasants had to work one month of every year digging deep channels for the water to irrigate the fertile land.

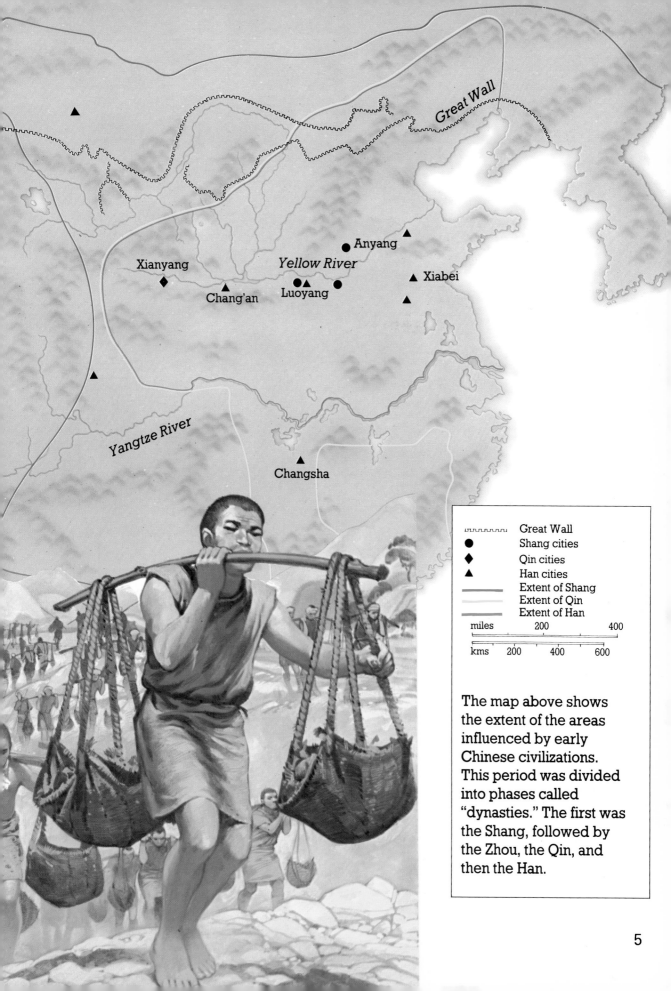

Great Wall

Anyang
Yellow River
Xianyang
Luoyang
Chang'an
Xiabei

Yangtze River

Changsha

	Great Wall
●	Shang cities
◆	Qin cities
▲	Han cities
	Extent of Shang
	Extent of Qin
	Extent of Han

miles 200 400

kms 200 400 600

The map above shows
the extent of the areas
influenced by early
Chinese civilizations.
This period was divided
into phases called
"dynasties." The first was
the Shang, followed by
the Zhou, the Qin, and
then the Han.

In Chinese legend, the Universe began as an egg, which one day split open. The top half became the sky, and the bottom half the Earth, and Pan Gu emerged. After 18,000 years, Pan Gu died and split into a number of parts. His head formed the Sun and Moon, his blood the rivers and seas, his sweat the rain, his breath the wind, and his fleas became the ancestors of mankind!

This design on a bronze mirror illustrates the Chinese symbols of world order. The Earth is represented by a square around a central knob. The T-shapes are the sacred mountains holding up the heavens, and the surrounding circles are the outer edges of the Universe.

The origins of China

The traditional Chinese view of the origins of their country moves from legend into historical fact. According to tradition, in the years before recorded history, there were a number of legendary rulers. First came Pan Gu, the Creator, followed by a series of emperors. They included Shen Nong, patron of agriculture and medicine, and the important "Yellow Emperor," famous for his wisdom of arts and sciences. The Xia dynasty, founded by Yu the Great, ends this mythical age.

The "Yellow Emperor," Huang Di, is regarded as the true founder of Chinese culture and ancestor of all emperors.

From fiction to fact

Legend now merges into historical fact with the appearance of the Shang – China's first important dynasty (1500–1028 BC). We have much historical evidence of the Shang and of their feudal society.

The "Divine Cultivator" or the first farmer, Shen Nong, is said to have ruled for 140 years.

According to legend Yu the "Great Engineer," founder of the mythical Xia dynasty, was the first man to control China's rivers. It is interesting that these legendary rulers seem to have concerned themselves with practical problems, rather than warfare.

7

A history of turbulence

It would seem that early Chinese dynasties followed a pattern. They would begin well, but decline after several generations of rulers, to be finally violently overthrown by a new leader and his armies.

The Shang began the tradition, prospering for five centuries, creating a culture that replaced the Stone Age with the Bronze Age and inventing a centralized kingdom. Eventually, their rule became unjust.

A nomadic people called the Zhou (1027-221BC) retaliated, causing the downfall of the Shang, and established a new dynasty. Zhou rulers made the feudal society more efficient. Land came under the control of nobles and rich peasants, causing frequent disputes. This period (475-221BC) is called the "Warring States" period.

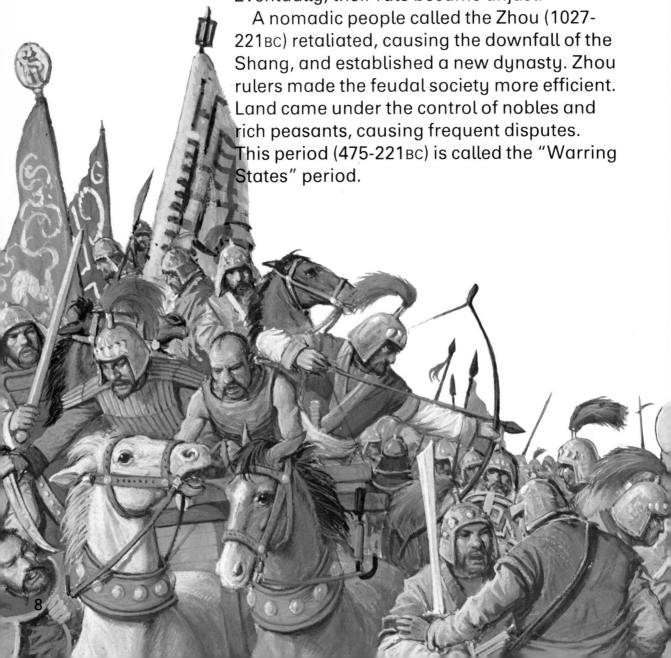

The Qin (221-206BC)

This period ended in the military triumph of the Qin. Although they ruled for only a short time, under their rule Chinese civilization began to really take shape. The Qin started a process of government that led to the country being unified into an empire for the first time.

Written language and laws were standardized. But the laws of the first Emperor, Shi Huang Di, were so harsh that rebellion broke out again, and Liu Bang and the armies of the Han emerged victorious.

The Han (202BC-AD220)

Han China became the greatest power in Asia and enjoyed long periods of peace. Prosperity reached a high peak and China became a great nation of traders, exporting goods like silk, spices, bronze and jade all over Asia and even into Europe.

The Shang army used curved bows, arrows, bronze daggers, axes and halberds – double-edged, pointed blades fixed to a shaft.

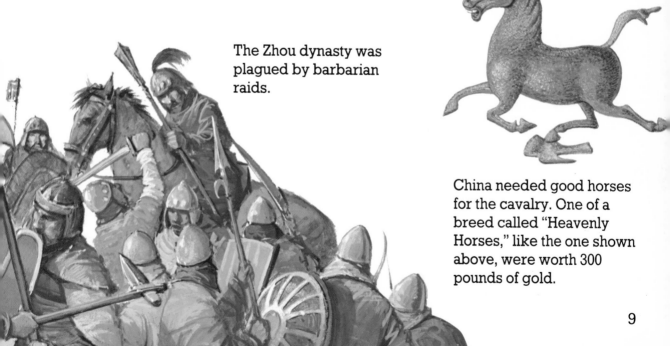

The Zhou dynasty was plagued by barbarian raids.

China needed good horses for the cavalry. One of a breed called "Heavenly Horses," like the one shown above, were worth 300 pounds of gold.

9

The Imperial Palace was surrounded by high walls for privacy. Life within was usually bound by elaborate ceremony. The Emperor's clothes, his food, even the design of the audience halls he sat in, were all chosen according to the seasons of the year.

In this scene we see the Emperor relaxing, watching a cockfight for amusement, with ladies of the court and other nobles. In the foreground, scholars and a court official, who wears an emblem on his cap indicating his rank, pass time in conversation.

Imperial life

Under the Han dynasty, the last traces of feudalism ended and the imperial era began. Society became more complicated, with a distinct class system. At the top of this structure was, of course, the Emperor. The early Chinese believed that the Emperor was given the authority to rule from Heaven, but that he had to deal justly with his people to keep his position.

The four classes

Kings and governors, appointed by the Emperor, were aided by the *shi* – state officials, nobles and scholars whose ability counted for more than birth. Next came the *nong*, the peasant farmers. Despite their poverty, they had social status because their work was vitally necessary – it supplied society's food. The work of the *gong*, the artisans who worked with precious stones and made weapons, was considered less important. Still lower were the *shang*, the merchants, perhaps because their great wealth constituted a threat to the princes who wanted to control the economy.

The social structure of Han China was clearly defined. The Emperor and his kings and governors ruled over the *shi, nong, gong* and *shang*. Soldiers who manned the frontiers were still lower in importance. It is perhaps an achievement of this early civilization that there was no large-scale slavery.

Governor

Emperor

King

Shi
State officials

Shi
Nobles and scholars

Nong Peasants

Soldiers

Shang
Merchants

Gong Artisans

Slaves

Chang'an

Chang'an was the well-planned capital of the later Han Empire. It was designed according to a set of ancient ideas about the order of the Universe and Nature.

Symbolism

The early Chinese believed that Heaven was round and that the Earth was square, and so the basic town plan was square accordingly. The city faced south, a direction associated with strength and the positive forces of Nature. Central and southern parts were occupied by the imperial palace, along with the houses of the nobles and official classes. The *gong*, the artisans, lived and worked in the north and west, while the *shang*, the despised merchant class, at first had to live outside the city walls. Thus, the whole structure of the city was a symbol of the physical universe and each man's place in it.

Walls and gates

The 24 km (15 miles) of tall outer walls contained straight, parallel streets. These were divided into 160 wards, or *li*. Each *li* was also walled, with a gate that was closed and guarded at night. The population, which consisted of some 246,000 people, was thus strictly controlled.

City life

As well as Chang'an, Imperial China had another great city – Luoyang, the capital of the earlier Han period, and there were also many large provincial towns. Several million people lived in these towns, which consequently must have been alive with activity. Early records criticize the extravagant way of life of the capital. In the nine market places of Chang'an, goods were briskly traded and passers-by would be entertained by puppet shows, musicians and gambling on cockfights.

In the market places, merchants and entertainers served courtiers, officials, scholars, soldiers and workmen, who jostled with beggars and thieves in the streets.

Government, commerce and learning

The capital was the seat of government, the commercial center for the Empire and also the center of learning. In 124 BC an Imperial University was established.

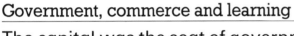

15

The peasantry

In the countryside, the self-supporting peasantry lived in one-room houses and worked from dawn to dusk, producing the country's food. In northern China, this was wheat or millet, grown on the terraces winding around the loess hillsides. In the south, they cultivated rice in an intricate patchwork of terraced and flooded paddy fields.

Large farms had water- and animal-powered mills and water-raising machinery. But the small farmers had to use very primitive methods, and although they had oxen and water buffalo, their life was hard.

Lasting achievements

The peasants also provided unpaid labor, building public works. Some of the more notable were: the Zheng guo Canal, which irrigated 400,000 acres; the Gong xian irrigation scheme, which is still in operation 2,000 years later; the Great Wall and over 32,000 km (20,000 miles) of road.

A prosperous farm. Our knowledge of these comes from models discovered in Han tombs.

Animal-drawn plow

Scythes

Threshing hammers

Wheelbarrows

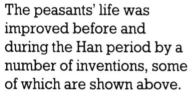
Communal building

Wood saws

The peasants' life was improved before and during the Han period by a number of inventions, some of which are shown above.

Terraced hillsides

Science and industry

By the end of the later Han dynasty, China led the world in technological development. As well as their achievements in controlling water, both for irrigation and transport, the salt and bronze industries were evidence of their considerable ingenuity. The Chinese were extracting ore, smelting it and casting it into weapons and tools about 1,700 years before Europe learned the technique. Iron was discovered in the fourth century BC, and became a state monopoly.

Salt was being mined in western China by 200BC. Bore-holes were drilled and salt water deep below the surface was drawn up into a tank. It was then carried along bamboo pipelines, to where the water was boiled away, leaving salt crystals. The heat might even have been produced by burning natural gas.

Silk production is China's oldest industry. Mulberry leaves were grown to feed to the silkworm grubs. Once the grubs had spun their silk cocoons, the insects were killed, and the delicate thread was carefully unwound onto reels and then spun into silk.

Silk production

Collecting mulberry leaves   Feeding the silkworms

18

Knowledge and inventions

The early Chinese also collected a mass of information. They discovered many of the basic principles of science – magnetism, for example. The Bureau of Astronomy regulated the calendar, measured the Moon's orbit around the Earth and charted over 1,100 stars. In medicine, acupuncture was appreciated as a method of healing. The Chinese also anticipated many discoveries thought to belong to the West.

Producing salt

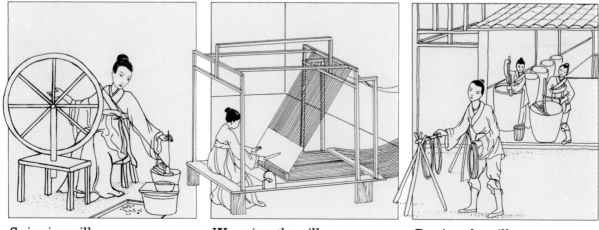

Spinning silk

Weaving the silk

Dyeing the silk

Art

Developments in the arts in Ancient China were usually linked to the demands of religion and ritual. Tombs have yielded a wealth of pottery figures, and elaborate carvings in marble, jade and ivory. But some of the most interesting finds are the richly ornamented bronze vessels, used in ancestor worship. Beautifully decorated with mythical beasts and formal patterns, these vessels are often inlaid with gold and silver figures.

The early history of bronze is a bit of a mystery, as there is no archaeological evidence of an experimental stage, before the sudden appearance of these sophisticated vessels.

A selection of early Chinese pottery

Silk, which was sold to the Romans in the later Han period, was woven into fabrics, used in embroidery, or, as in the picture above, was used as a canvas to paint on.

20

Art of the Imperial Age

Beautiful lacquered tables, boxes, trays and dishes furnished many Han tombs. Lacquerware, which is strong but extremely light, is an early Chinese invention. It was made by covering a thin base of carved wood with many coats of lacquer – the resin of a native sumac tree – which built up a hard surface that could then be painted.
Some tombs were decorated with engraved or painted pottery slabs, showing real and imaginary scenes.

This is a fifth century BC bronze doorknocker. It uses the "monster mask" – one of the best-known Shang motifs.

Casting a bronze ritual food vessel

Belief

A number of distinct ways of thinking emerged in Ancient China, which were destined to shape the civilization for 2,000 years. Although these "philosophies" were seemingly contradictory, they could exist in harmony in the Chinese mind.

The "two ways"

Alongside primitive religions, schools of thought emerged to cope with the problems of morality and truth. Two that were to become the main currents of Chinese thought were Confucianism and Taoism, based on the teachings of Confucius and Laozi.

Confucius (551-479 BC) taught a practical way of life, based on loyalty to the family, ancestor worship and obedience to the laws of society. His philosophy put emphasis on ceremonies and order.

Yin and Yang

The Chinese believed that the harmony of the Universe depended on a balance between the forces of Yin and Yang. Yin represented everything negative, female, dark and of the Earth. Yang was positive, male, light and of Heaven. The forces were visualized as a circle divided into two equal parts by a curved line, expressing the idea of a delicate balance.

Laozi, founder of Taoism

Taoism

Taoism, which included many of the gods worshipped in earlier times, taught that men should always work in harmony with nature, never against it. Taoists believed in a "natural" way to truth, rather than in an ordered government of laws and rigid authority. Confucianism and Taoism are both opposite and yet complementary, and the educated Chinese of the time would have tried to live by both.

Legalism and Buddhism

A less enduring philosophy flourished briefly under the Qin dynasty – legalism. Rather than relying on improving human nature, legalists concentrated on man's imperfections and advised strict laws and punishments.

Buddhism was not well-established in China during the Han dynasty, but Buddhist beliefs had begun to filter in from India. Eventually, Confucianism, Taoism and Buddhism were regarded as "three ways to one goal."

Confucius teaching his disciples

Relaxation

Children and adults enjoyed board games like *liu bo*, played by throwing sticks and moving pieces around the board.

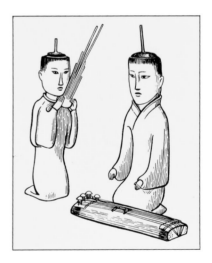

The early Chinese enjoyed music. One of these wooden figures is a panpipes player and the other has a three-stringed zither.

Seasonal celebrations and festivals included firework displays and spectacles of kite flying.

Family life

The family was the most important institution in China. All Chinese homes had a special altar, where the family would pray to the spirits of their dead ancestors. It was thought that the living and the dead were interdependent – the spirits needed offerings and the living needed their blessings.

The trappings of wealth

Rich families wore silk and expensive jewelry, and feasted on exotic dishes. They ate snails in vinegar, dog meat and tangerines, and drank wine, coconut milk and fermented palm juice. Embroidered cushions, carpets, paintings and lacquered tables decorated their homes.

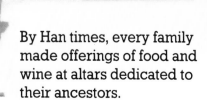

By Han times, every family made offerings of food and wine at altars dedicated to their ancestors.

Preparations for eternity

A lot of our information about early Chinese civilization comes from archaeological investigations of the tombs of the period. The dead were buried with much ritual and ceremony. Tombs were hewn from solid rock, or built of stone or brick and covered with an earthen mound.

The burial suit of Liu Sheng, a Han prince, was made of 2,000 separate squares of jade, a stone that supposedly preserved the body. When discovered, of course, it contained nothing but dust.

Shang burials

Shang nobles were buried with bronze vessels for the spirit's needs, carriages for his transportation and real people for his servants! It was thought that the dead should be accompanied by people and objects that would be useful to them in the afterlife.

Zhou and Han burials

Zhou rulers ended human sacrifice, but continued to bury valuable objects. In Han times, however, these were replaced by specially made models. Pottery figures and bronze miniatures of horses and chariots took the place of their living counterparts.

Remembrance ceremonies

Deaths were remembered in periodic rituals. If the death was recent, a young member of the family was dressed to impersonate the ancestor and offered wine and meat from an animal sacrifice. In this way, the family could expect the ancestor's blessings.

The funeral of Liu Sheng was an elaborate affair. He and his wife were buried in twin tombs, containing 3,000 precious objects.

The terracotta army

In 1974, the mausoleum of the First Emperor, Shi Huang Di, was discovered. This tomb is magnificent, partly because of its monumental scale (the ground plan suggests the layout of an ideal imperial city), but mainly for the eerily lifelike, life-sized terracotta army that guards it.

One of the underground chambers discovered contains over 6,000 figures arranged in military formation. In another, 1,400 chariots and cavalrymen were unearthed, while in a third, figures representing an elite command force were found.

No two alike

Each figure was individually modeled and carved. Different uniforms, armor and elaborate hairstyles distinguish the warriors from each other. No two faces are alike, and they even show different expressions.

The terracotta army is evidence of the power of the Emperor, who is said to have led "a million armored soldiers, a thousand chariots and ten thousand horses to conquer and gloat over the world."

On the left we see the head and shoulders of a Qin general. Originally the entire army was painted.

The terracotta army was created over 2,000 years ago, to serve the first Emperor of the Qin dynasty in his afterlife.

Past and present

The Great Wall of China, built over 2,000 years ago, and visited by thousands of tourists each year, is the only manmade edifice to be seen from the Moon.

Today, the Chinese rightly see themselves as the direct descendants of the ancient civilization. They have been deeply influenced by, and owe much to, its long history. Unlike so many countries in the world today, the frontiers of China changed little over the last 2,000 years. Inventions of early China contributed to world civilization, and the early philosophies played an important part in forming the Chinese character. Moreover, the political structure established under the Han dynasty set a pattern that was to serve China until 1911, when the last dynasty was overthrown.

"Let the past serve the present"

With these words, Mao Zedong, leader of the People's Republic, admitted the importance of early China to the modern day. He encouraged archaeological investigations, which will continue to add to our knowledge of one of the most fascinating civilizations on Earth.

Glossary

Acupuncture A method of healing by piercing the skin at certain points with needles.

Archaeology The scientific study of historical remains.

Barbarians The early Chinese referred to *anyone* outside their borders as a barbarian. Even in the 19th century Europeans were still called "barbarians."

Feudalism A social system, based on land ownership, in which peasants and slaves were ruled over by the court and nobles.

Irrigation The supplying of land with water, by means of channels or streams.

Loess A rich, yellow earth that covers the land around the Yellow River.

Primitive religions The early Chinese worshipped their ancestors and the gods of Nature.

State monopoly When a government keeps total control of an industry.

Index

A armies 8-9, 28-9
art 20-1

B beliefs 6-7, 12, 22-3
bronze 8-9, 18, 20-1
Buddhism 23

C cities 5, 12-15
clothes 25, 27
Confucius 22-3

D dynasties 5, 7-9

E education 14
emperors 7, 9-11, 28
entertainment 10, 14, 24

F farming 16-17
food 16, 25

G government 9, 14
Great Wall 4-5, 16, 30

H houses 13, 25

I industries 18
inventions 17-19, 21
iron 18

L Laozi 22
legalism 23

P Pan Gu 6-7
peasants 4, 8, 11, 16-17
philosophers 22-3

R religions 22-3, 25
rivers 4-5, 6

S salt 18
science 19
Shen Nong 7
silk 9, 18-20
social structure 11-12

T Taoism 22-3
tombs 16, 20-1, 26-8
trade 9, 14

W weapons 9, 11, 18

Y "Yellow Emperor" 7
Yin and Yang 22
Yu The Great 7

PRINTED IN BELGIUM BY

proost
INTERNATIONAL BOOK PRODUCTION